The TRUEST HEART KEEPSAKE

Writing and Illustrating Your Strengths

by Jayne Sbarboro

THE TRUEST HEART COMPANION
Writing and Illustrating Your Strengths

All rights reserved by the author.

No portion of this book may be reproduced in any form, stored in any retrieval system, or transmitted in any form by any means—electronic, mechanical, photocopying, recording or otherwise without written permission of the author, except as provided by U.S. copyright law.

Teachers are granted special permission for use,
but should contact the author
through the publisher's website **before copying**.
Contact to be made through info@TruestHeart.com

The author wants student samples to create a bank of examples on the website for other children to use to recognize and build their strengths.

TRUEST HEART is a registered trademark.

ISBN 978-0-9992420-6-3

1. Bullying   2. Self Esteem

Copyright 2019
Montgomery Publishing Co.
All rights reserved.

Good things come to those who wait—

but better things come to those who try.

No matter how many mistakes you make, or how slow your progress... you are still way ahead of everyone ...who is not trying.

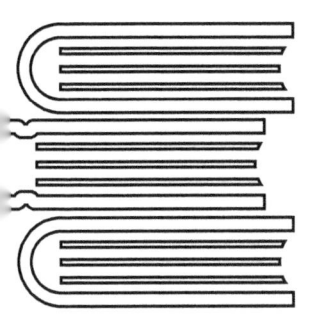

It does not matter how slowly you go, As long as you DO NOT STOP.

I tried _____.

Every effort I make increases my endurance.

Draw what this looks like in action.
Use either words or pictures. Give an example of a time that you kept going…

_____

_____

_____

One day
you will tell
your story
of how you overcame
what you went through...
And it will become
someone
else's
SURVIVAL GUIDE.

I practiced being brave when I _____
_____.

... I keep practicing to control my fear.

What could this look like in practice? Use words or pictures to create a visual image or tell a story of when you practiced bravery.

You have two hands.

One is for helping yourself

...and one is for helping others.

I was generous when I
_____
_____.

...giving to others makes me feel good inside.
   I believe good things will happen to me.

Visualize yourself giving to another. It might have been a compliment, a gift, a touch, or even just the benefit of the doubt. Use words or a drawing to create the visual image of a time when you practiced generosity.

I was creative when I
_____.

Being creative makes my heart more flexible.

Use words or pictures. Give a visualize example…

_____
_____
_____

BOREDOM

is not the worst thing in the world.

Boredom is the SPACE YOU NEED to create something different.

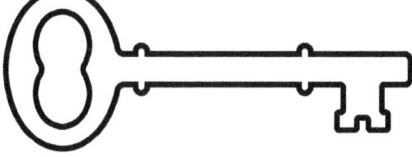

I am curious about

If you
are unwilling to learn,
no one can help you.

If you are determined to learn, no one can STOP you.

Being curious opens my mind to new things!

CREATING FRIENDSHIPS

_____ is a friend who is different from me.

I like people who are different from me because:

♡ I get to care about more people.

♡ They have strengths that I get to learn.

♡ They have different ideas that help me.

♡ Caring about people makes my heart happy.

Friends are different from me
 and there are many ways they are the same as me.

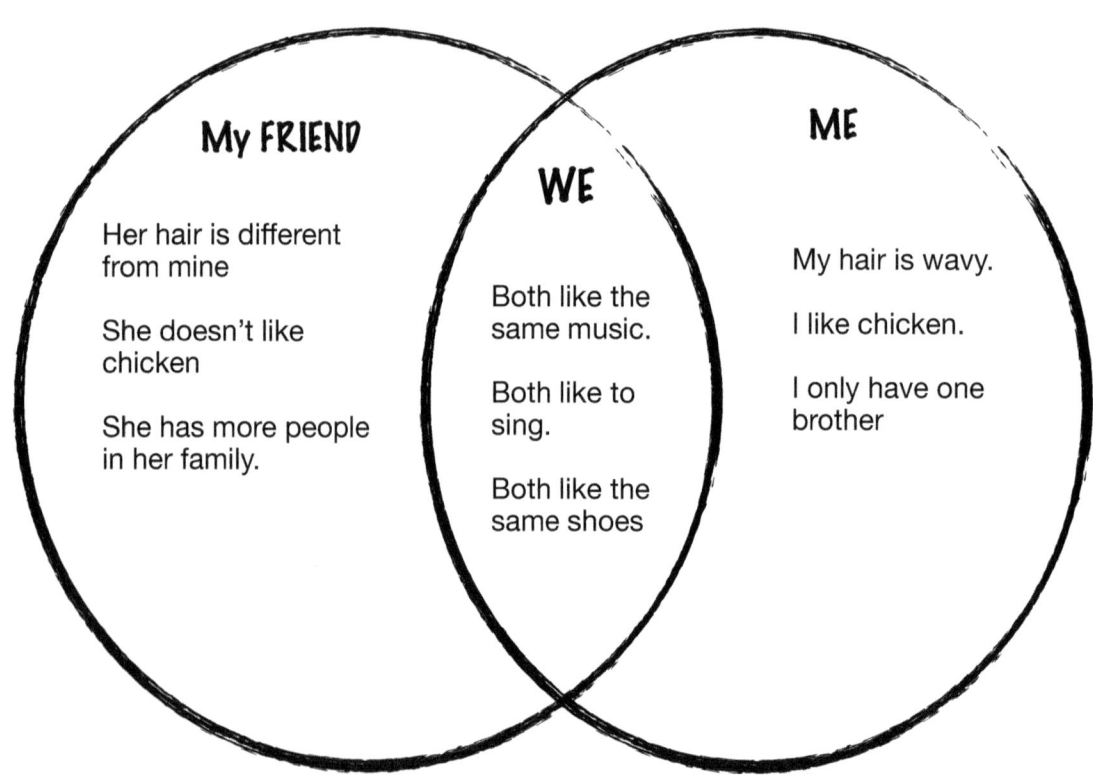

My FRIEND

Her hair is different from mine

She doesn't like chicken

She has more people in her family.

WE

Both like the same music.

Both like to sing.

Both like the same shoes

ME

My hair is wavy.

I like chicken.

I only have one brother

FRIENDSHIP

Liking other people makes my heart feel BIGGER.

Here are some ways we are different

...and some ways we are the same:

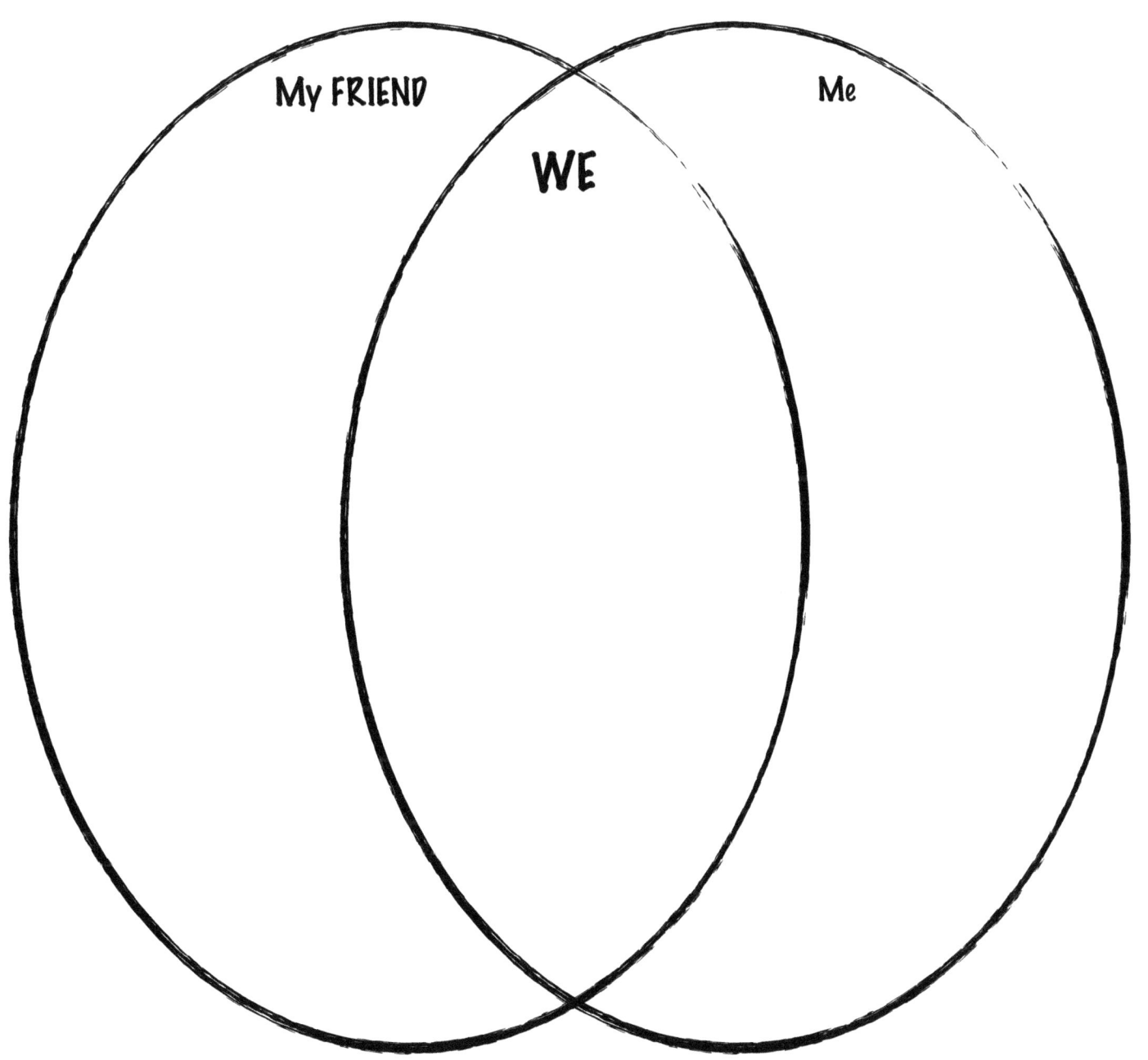

KIND WORDS AND DEEDS

When I give you something, whether it's a compliment or a gift,
I raise you up:

"Hey! I like how you are generous to other"

"Wow. Thanks!"

A good friend gives back. They raise me up too—to be equal to them.

"I noticed you helped that other kid. That was really nice."

"Hey. Thanks"

...We do it again. Boom! **It's FUN! Up they go!**

...Back to me. **Boom! SO FUN! Up I go!**

WE BOTH GET TO FEEL GREAT!

All good relationships are equal.

USING KIND WORDS AND DEEDS

Ask as many people as you can to give you ideas on how to be uplifting to others:

1.

2.

3.

4.

5.

6.

7.

LEARNING TO BE AN ALLY

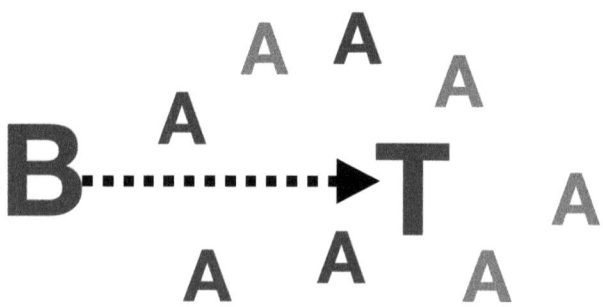

This is a diagram of kids standing around.

The person doing the **B**ullying Behavior is on the left.
See them shooting unkindness at the other kid?

Over on the right is the **T**arget.

….Of course the Target is upset because of the bullying behavior.

All around are **A**udience.

Every person who hears or sees bullying behavior
    Is automatically an **A**udience to the actions.

The **A**udience hears what is going on.
    ….Maybe they have seen it happen before.

But each Audience makes a choice…
    to be an **Ally** or an **Adversary.**

I BECOME AN ALLY

If I do nothing, then I *look* like I'm an **Adversary**.
That means the **child doing the bullying** thinks I am on *their* side.

> I might be afraid to speak up. I don't want the Bully to shoot unkindness at me.
> **But *staying quiet* puts me on the side of the Bullying behavior.**
>
> **I don't want to be their side.**

If I just stand nearer the Target, I show the Target my support.
> I could also walk away with the Target to stop the meanness.
>
> **If I say something or *do something*, then I become an ALLY**

I may not know it, and sometimes it may not seem like it, but
the team of Allies is always bigger
> than any **B**ullying behavior.

> **I can be an ALLY — I *will* make a difference.**
> I might not be able to do everything, but I can do something.
> And **I promise myself to do something**.

Here are some ways I will do:

1) _____

2) _____

3) _____

Kindfulness

FOCUSING OUR **FULL ATTENTION** ON HELPING OTHERS.

www.ingramcontent.com/pod-product-compliance
Lightning Source LLC
Chambersburg PA
CBHW061156010526
44118CB00027B/2993